D1371096

Investigating
Weather

Miriam Coleman

PowerKiDS
press.

New York

Published in 2016 by The Rosen Publishing Group, Inc.
29 East 21st Street, New York, NY 10010

First Edition

Editor: Sarah Machajewski
Book Design: Katelyn Heinle

Photo Credits: Cover, p. 7 (tornado) Minerva Studio/Shutterstock.com; p. 5 Patrick Foto/Shutterstock.com; p. 7 (sunny) S. Borisov/ Shutterstock.com; p. 7 (hurricane) B747/Shutterstock.com; p. 7 (snowstorm) Igumnova Irina/Shutterstock.com; p. 9 Alex Staroseltsev/ Shutterstock.com; p. 11 Jim Reed/Science Source/Getty Images; p. 13 (water cycle) Merkushev Vasiliy/Shutterstock.com; p. 13 (cirrus) Pi-Lens/Shutterstock.com; p. 13 (stratus) Wildnerdpix/Shutterstock.com; p. 13 (cumulonimbus) kazoka/Shutterstock.com; p. 14 kavram/Shutterstock.com; p. 15 Kim Steele/Photodisc/Getty Images; p. 17 ekler/Shutterstock.com; p. 19 (thermometer) Feng Yu/Shutterstock.com; p. 19 (barometer) GlOck/Shutterstock.com; p. 19 (rain gauge) Laurell, Philip/Getty Images; p. 19 (wind vane) albund/Shutterstock.com; p. 19 (anemometer) Cico/Shutterstock.com; p. 19 (weather balloon) Armin Rose/ Shutterstock.com; p. 19 (satellite) Science & Society Picture Library/SSPL/Getty Images; p. 20 Carolina K. Smith MD/ Shutterstock.com; p. 21 Bloomberg/Bloomberg/Getty Images; p. 22 M G Therin Weise/Photographer's Choice RF/Getty Images.

Library of Congress Cataloging-in-Publication Data

Coleman, Miriam.
Investigating weather / by Miriam Coleman.
p. cm. — (Earth science detectives)
Includes index.
ISBN 978-1-4777-5959-2 (pbk.)
ISBN 978-1-4777-5960-8 (6-pack)
ISBN 978-1-4777-5958-5 (library binding)
1. Weather — Juvenile literature. 2. Meteorology — Juvenile literature. I. Coleman, Miriam. II. Title.
QC981.3 C65 2015
551.5—d23

Manufactured in the United States of America

CPSIA Compliance Information: Batch #WS15PK: For Further Information contact Rosen Publishing, New York, New York at 1-800-237-9932

CONTENTS

READING WEATHER CLUES

Weather is always around us, even when we can't see it. It has a great effect on our lives. It **determines** what we wear, what we can or can't do outside, and more. Weather is important, and there's much to be learned from it.

Meteorologists (mee-tee-uh-RAH-luh-jihsts) are scientists who study weather. Meteorologists are like detectives who gather clues from weather all over the world. They put these clues together to learn why weather acts the way it does, how weather has changed over time, and what kind of weather Earth may have in the future.

Rain is just one of our planet's many kinds of weather.

WHAT IS WEATHER?

Weather is the conditions around us at a particular place and time. Weather makes it hot or chilly, wet or dry, sunny or cloudy, and windy or calm. Warm, sunny days are weather, but so are thunderstorms, **blizzards**, and **tornadoes**. Rain, fog, ice storms, heat waves, **hurricanes**, and hail are all forms of weather, too.

At any moment, weather is different in different parts of the world. The weather can even be different just a mile away. Weather can also change very quickly. Bright sunny skies can turn into stormy weather within hours or even minutes.

CLUE ME IN

Blizzards, tornadoes, and hurricanes are considered **extreme** weather. Extreme weather is any condition that poses danger to people or isn't common for an area.

These images show just some of the kinds of weather meteorologists study. Each kind **reveals** something about the conditions in that place at that time.

IT'S ALL IN THE ATMOSPHERE

Meteorologists know they must study the atmosphere in order to learn about weather. Earth's atmosphere is a blanket of gases around the planet. The atmosphere traps some of the sun's heat to keep Earth warm enough so life can grow. It also keeps Earth from getting too much heat.

The atmosphere is made of several **layers**. The troposphere is nearest to Earth. It reaches a height of about 11 miles (18 km) above Earth's surface. Most of Earth's weather occurs here. The stratosphere is the next layer. It reaches a height of about 30 miles (48 km).

CLUE ME IN

The stratosphere contains a layer of a gas called ozone that blocks much of the sun's harmful rays from reaching Earth.

EARTH'S ATMOSPHERE

STRATOSPHERE

TROPOSPHERE

Most of Earth's weather occurs in the troposphere and stratosphere. Little to no weather happens in the other layers.

ELEMENTS OF WEATHER

Weather includes six main elements: temperature, air **pressure**, wind, humidity, clouds, and precipitation. Temperature is the measurement of how cold or hot the atmosphere is. Air pressure is the force created by the weight of the air. Wind is the movement of air.

Humidity is the amount of water vapor in the atmosphere. Clouds form when tiny droplets of water vapor stick together. When the water droplets inside a cloud stick together and form large droplets, they fall from the sky as precipitation. Meteorologists have learned that different combinations of these elements create different kinds of weather.

This meteorologist is measuring the speed of the wind. His measurements will give him an idea of what's happening in the atmosphere over that part of Earth.

CLUE ME IN

Precipitation is rain, snow, sleet, or hail that forms in clouds and falls to the ground.

THE WATER CYCLE

Water has everything to do with weather, so scientists study how water moves on, above, and below Earth's surface through a **process** called the water cycle.

The water cycle begins with evaporation, which is when the sun heats the water in oceans, rivers, and lakes and turns it into water vapor. Next is condensation, when water vapor in the air cools and comes together to form clouds. Precipitation happens when the air becomes heavy with water droplets. The water falls from the sky as rain, snow, sleet, or hail. When rain falls or snow and ice melt, the water collects in bodies of water until it evaporates again.

The water cycle creates many kinds of clouds. Clouds are clues about different kinds of weather. Light, puffy clouds are a sign of good weather, while flat or dark clouds may mean light rain or bad storms.

cirrus

stratus

cumulonimbus

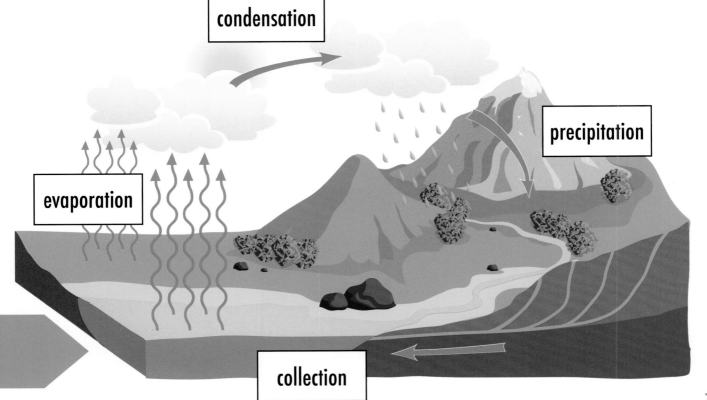

condensation

precipitation

evaporation

collection

13

WEATHER FRONTS

The movement of air masses affects the weather just as much as the movement of water. The meeting of a lighter, warmer air mass with a heavier, cooler air mass often causes storms. The border between two different air masses is called a front.

A cold front occurs when cold air pushes into a mass of warmer air. Cold fronts move fast and cause sudden drops in temperature as well as heavy rain, thunder, and lightning. Warm fronts occur when a warm air mass pushes into a cold air mass. Warm fronts can bring clouds and wet weather. They also cause snow and freezing rain in the winter.

CLUE ME IN
Warm air fronts move slowly, which means bad weather can last for several days.

Meteorologists are able to track air masses several days before they reach an area and **predict** what the weather will be like once they arrive. This gives us time to prepare for cold temperatures, lots of rain, or a beautiful, sunny day.

Everything scientists have learned about weather has helped us understand Earth's **climate**. Scientists have gathered so much **data** that we can use findings from the past to find out what the weather will be like in a place during certain times of the year.

An area's climate is affected by where it is on Earth and how much sunlight it gets. The climate affects the types of plants and animals that can live in an area. Tropical climates have high temperatures all year and often have lots of rain. Polar climates are freezing most of the year. Temperate climates have warm, dry summers and cool, wet winters.

CLUE ME IN

Earth is split into three main climate zones, or areas. The zones are determined by temperature and how much rainfall there is.

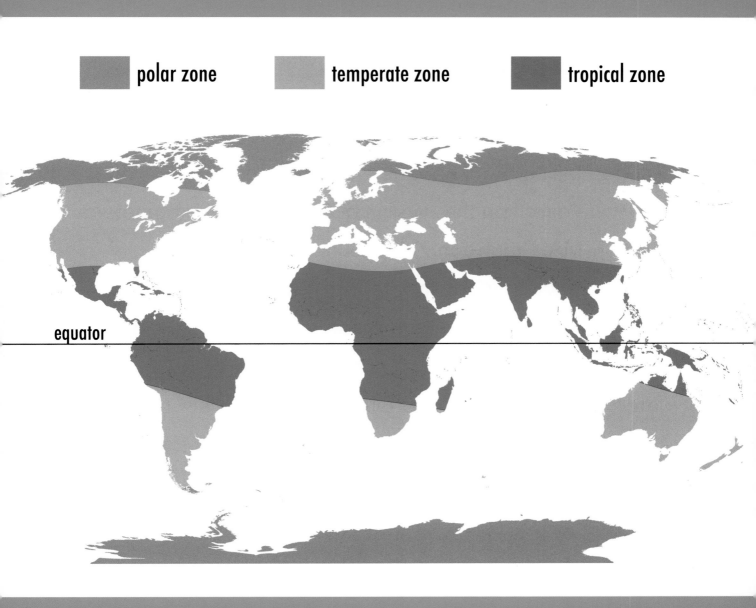

polar zone　　temperate zone　　tropical zone

equator

Earth's climate is always changing. Some clues that may reveal climate change are an increased number of storms in an area, more tornadoes, a lack of rain or precipitation, or weather that's colder or hotter than normal.

TOOLS TO FIND CLUES

Scientists have created many different tools for measuring weather. Thermometers measure temperature. Barometers measure air pressure and tell us whether it's rising or falling. Rain gauges measure rainfall. Wind vanes show the direction the wind is blowing, and anemometers (aa-nuh-MAH-muh-tuhrz) measure wind speed.

Weather balloons fly into the stratosphere to collect data about air pressure, temperature, and humidity. Some tools can find rain, hail, and snow in the air. Weather satellites, or machines that circle Earth to collect data, are another tool meteorologists use. They track Earth's temperature and moisture from space, creating images that are sent back to Earth to be studied.

The weather is no match for scientists armed with these tools. They each teach us something different about how weather acts and how it affects Earth.

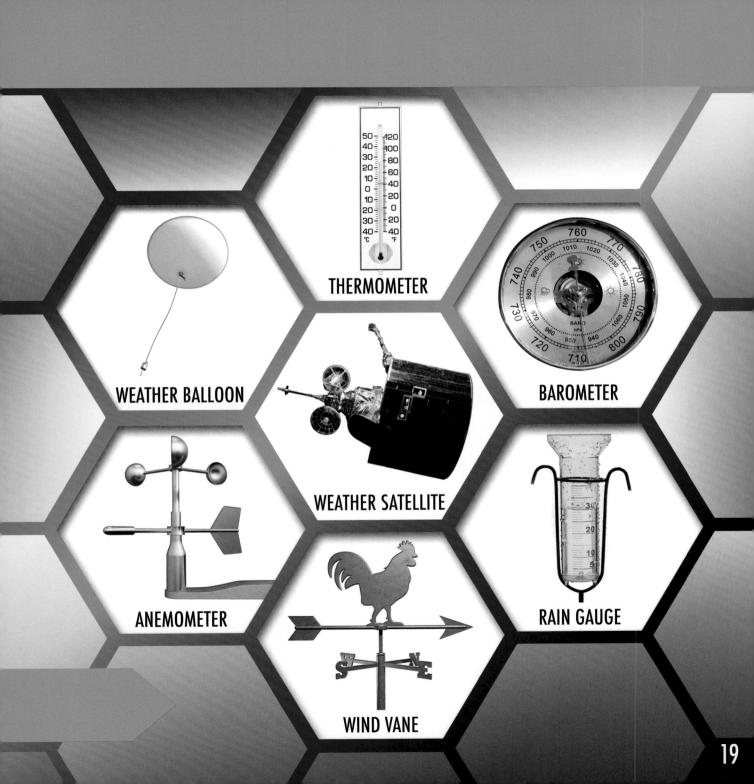

THERMOMETER

WEATHER BALLOON

BAROMETER

WEATHER SATELLITE

ANEMOMETER

RAIN GAUGE

WIND VANE

FORECASTING

After using their tools to measure weather, meteorologists study the data to learn what's happening with weather near and far. This helps them determine how weather moves and changes throughout an area.

Meteorologists use powerful computers to create weather maps. The computers can process huge amounts of data at once to show what the weather is likely to do. Using these methods, meteorologists can predict what the weather will be like in an hour, the next day, or the next week. This is called a weather forecast. Meteorologists aren't always correct, however, since weather often changes at a moment's notice!

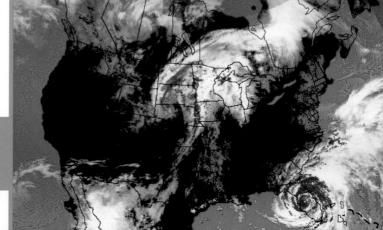

This weather map shows a hurricane in the bottom right corner, just over Florida.

Weather maps and forecasts help all kinds of people. Pilots and ship captains use them to stay safe when they're flying or sailing. You may listen to a weather forecast before taking a trip to the beach.

Scientists have found **evidence** showing Earth's climate is changing because of human activity. In fact, 97 percent of scientists think climate change in the past 100 years has largely been caused by people.

Changes to Earth's climate have caused glaciers to melt, seas to rise, global temperatures to increase, and more. This can be harmful to plants, animals, and people. It's important to learn how to read clues that show us how weather acted in the past and what it will do in the future. These clues will help us understand what makes the climate change and what we

can do to help keep Earth healthy.

GLOSSARY

blizzard: A winter storm with blowing snow and strong winds.

climate: The weather conditions in an area over a long period of time.

data: Facts gathered for study.

determine: To cause something to occur in a particular way.

evidence: Facts, signs, or information that proves something to be true.

extreme: Very serious.

hurricane: A storm with strong spinning winds that forms over warm water.

layer: One thickness lying over or under another.

predict: To make a guess, based on facts, about what will happen in the future.

pressure: A force that pushes on something else.

process: A series of actions or steps. Also, to perform a series of steps.

reveal: To make known.

tornado: A spinning column of wind that reaches from a cloud to the ground.

INDEX

WEBSITES

Due to the changing nature of Internet links, PowerKids Press has developed an online list of websites related to the subject of this book. This site is updated regularly. Please use this link to access the list: www.powerkidslinks.com/det/wthr